PIZZAPEDIA

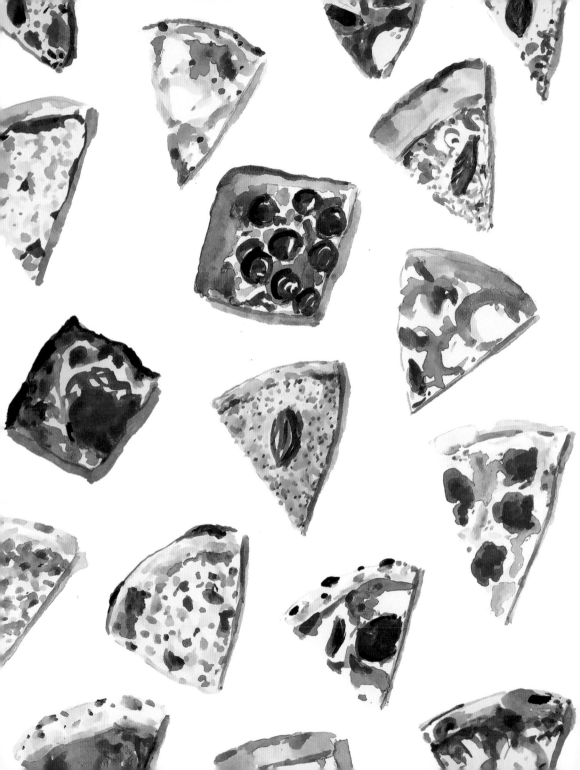

PIZZAPEDIA

An illustrated guide to everyone's favorite food

DAN BRANSFIELD

TEN SPEED PRESS
California | New York

CONTENTS

3.75

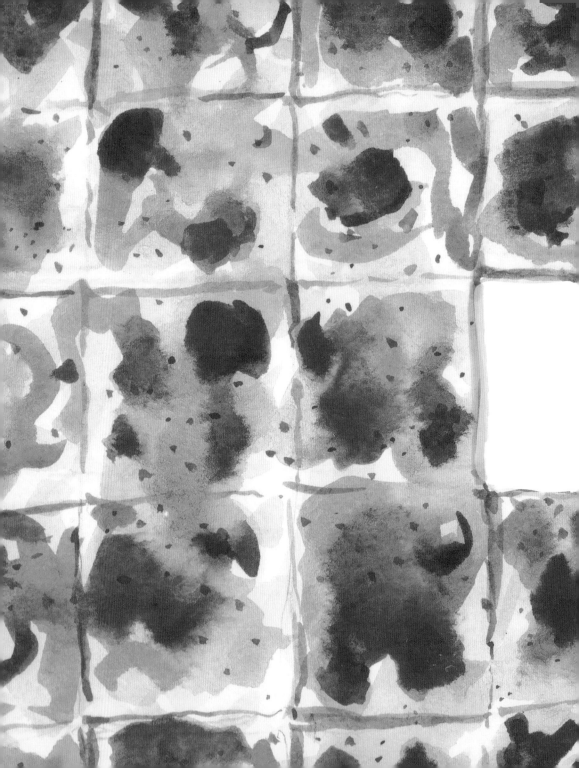

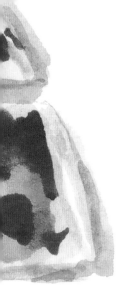

INTRO

A brief reflection
on my early
(and often stormy)
relationship with pizza.

THE BEGINNING

Some of my earliest memories regarding pizza involve spending Saturday nights at home, in Oak Park, Illinois, with my brothers and sisters. We would watch "The Love Boat" and "Fantasy Island" and order pizza from neighborhood places like Capizi's, Salerno's, and Grand Slam.

3

Our pizza nights were not without incident. On occasion, when I'd bite into a slice, the cheese would slide off.

"My pizza broke!" I'd exclaim.

My siblings would put the cheese back on, but I was inconsolable—I could not be convinced to eat that mishapen slice.

These pizza nights happened with an assured regularity.
But time marches on. The house in Oak Park would
change hands over time. Capizi's would shutter
and "The Love Boat" would sail only in reruns.

But the one thing that remains reliably
constant and immune to the ravages
of time is pizza — which I love to
this very day.

I just don't cry as much now
when the cheese falls off.

ORIGINS

The development of pizza from ancient flat breads to the modern margherita.

5TH CENTURY B.C.

At the height of the Persian Empire, it is said that the soldiers of Darius the Great (521–486 B.C.), accustomed to lengthy marches, baked a kind of bread covered with cheese and dates right on their shields.

A.D. 79

A proto-pizza oven and loaf of bread
from The House of Pansa, Pompeii.
The bakery and dwelling were initially
excavated in 1810.

The term "pizza" first appeared in a Latin text from the southern Italian town of Gaeta in A.D. 997. The text states that a tenant of certain property is to give the bishop of Gaeta "duodecim pizze" (twelve pizzas) every Christmas and another twelve every Easter Sunday.

A major ingredient of the pizza arrives in Europe in the 16th century, when the Conquistadors bring tomatoes back from the New World—but it would take another two centuries after the tomatoes' introduction to become widely accepted in Europe.

The tomato was slow to be embraced in the kitchen as it was thought to be a poisonous member of the nightshade family, the frequently toxic group that also includes tobacco, henbane, and mandrake. John Gerard, author of an influential 16th-century herbal, believed the fruits to be "of ranke and stinking savour," offering "very little nourishment to the body, and the same naught and corrupt." It would take about 200 years for "the golden apple" to find its way into Italian cuisine.

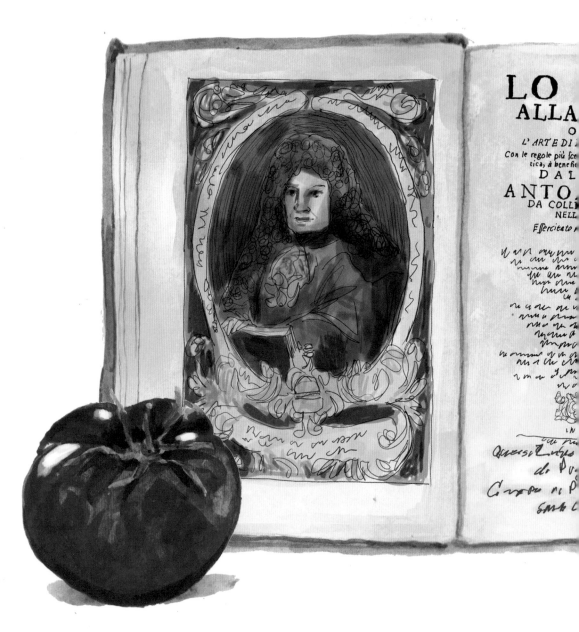

LO SCALCO ALLA MODERNA, written by Antonio Latini, chef to the Spanish Viceroy of Naples, was the first Italian cookbook to include tomato sauce. One recipe calls for sauce "alla spagnola" (in the Spanish style)—a sauce closer to salsa.

MARGHERITA OF SAVOY

In 1889, the "pizza Margherita" was named after Margherita of Savoy, Queen consort of Italy, while visiting Naples with her husband, King Umberto I.

UMBERTO I

The "pizza Umberto," alas, never quite took off.

PIZZERIA

NAPLES

is traditionally credited as the home of modern pizza with the opening of Antica Pizzeria Port'Alba in 1830.

Antica Pizzeria Port'Alba
The first pizzeria in Naples.

"Pizza a Portafoglio"

Pizzeria Port'Alba has been serving this popular wood-fired pizza ever since it first opened in 1830.

The simple pizza is meant to be folded like a wallet, or "portafoglio," and eaten on the go.

In the 1700s, Neapolitan sailors began topping their bread with tomatoes and herbs on their long voyages, giving rise to "pizza alla marinara."

PIZZERIA
53½
NAPOLETANA

GENNARO LOMBARDI

Although Gennaro Lombardi was influenced by the pies of Naples, he was forced to adapt pizza to Americans. The wood-fired ovens and **mozzarella di bufala** were substituted with coal-powered ovens and **fior di latte**, initiating the evolution of the American Pie.

Pizza in America was mostly limited to Italian immigrant communities until after World War II. Much of pizza's popularity in America is attributed to soldiers returning home from Italy after the war.

1954 • Shakey's Pizza Parlor
The first franchise pizza chain in the United States,
founded in Sacramento, CA, by Sherwood "Shakey" Johnson.

Chuck E. Cheese's Pizza Time Theatre

first opened in San Jose, California, on May 17, 1977.
It was the first family restaurant to combine food, video
games, and animatronics. The franchise filed for bankruptcy
in 1984, and was bought by competitor ShowBiz Pizza Place.

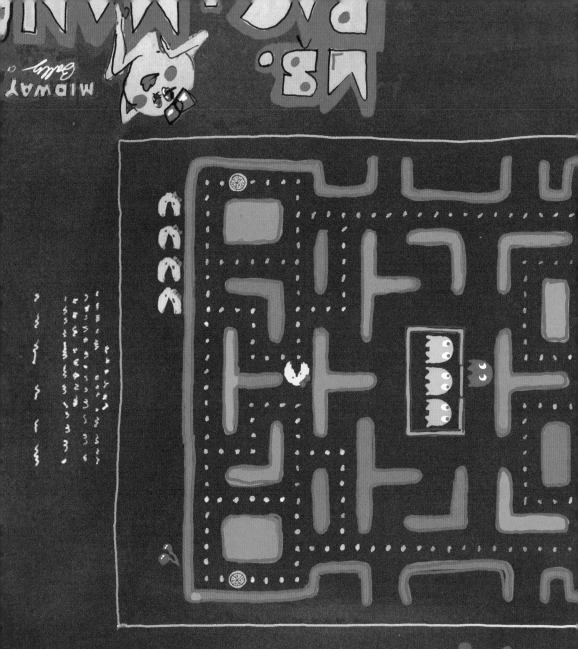

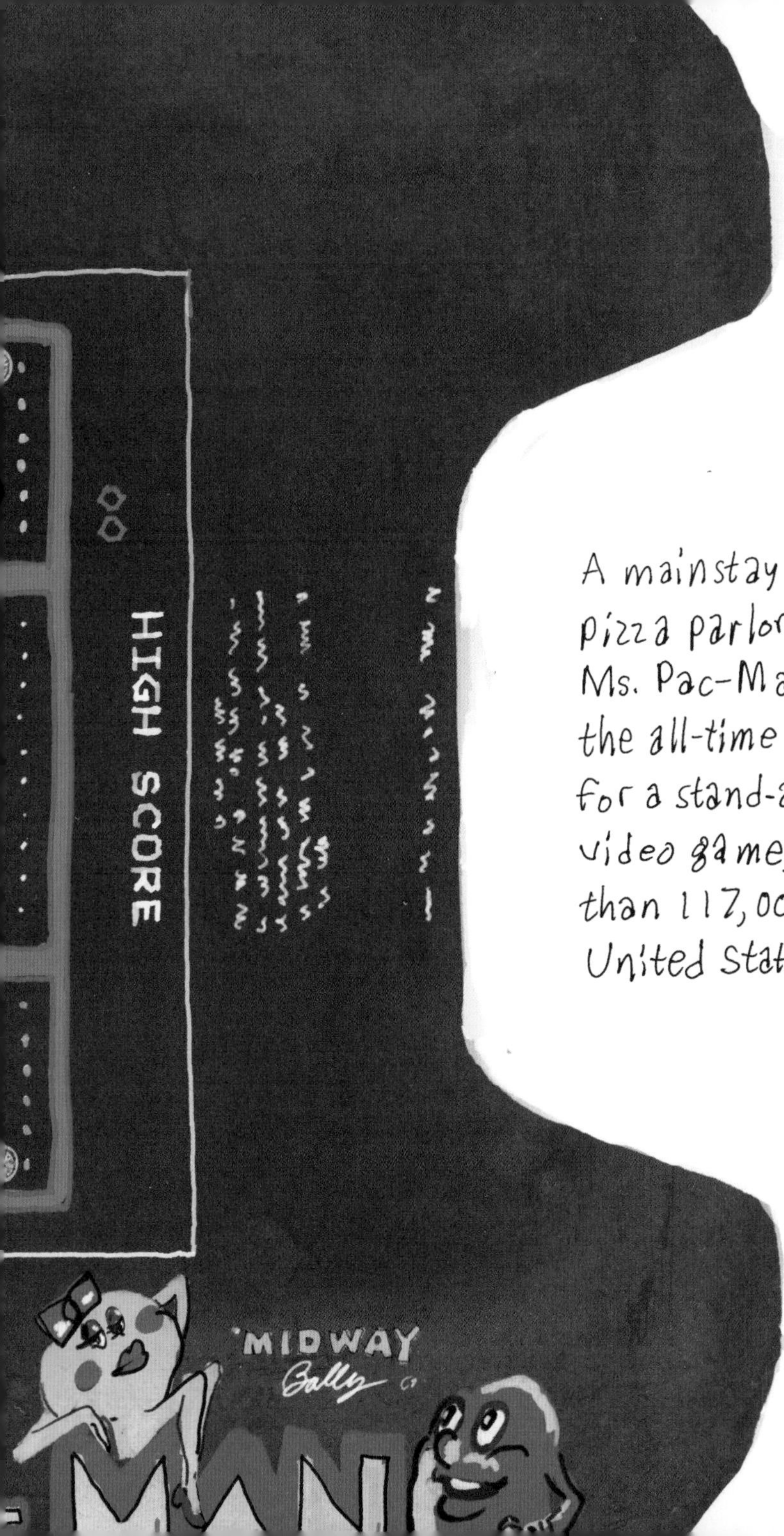

HIGH SCORE

A mainstay in American pizza parlors in the '80s, Ms. Pac-Man still holds the all-time sales record for a stand-alone arcade video game, selling more than 117,000 units in the United States.

'MIDWAY Bally co

VARIATIONS

The many styles of pizza, from the traditional New York slice to the unconventional vending-machine pies.

NEW YORK STYLE

This pizza, with its thin, pliable crust, is traditionally made in coal-fired ovens with a dry, low-moisture mozzerella, ideal for the oven's high heat.

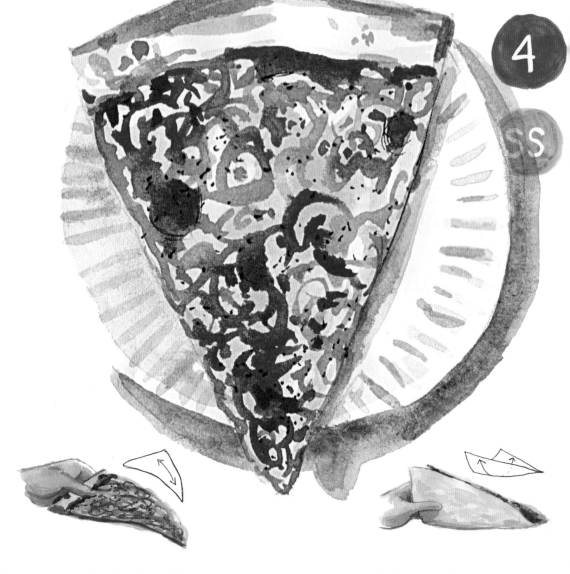

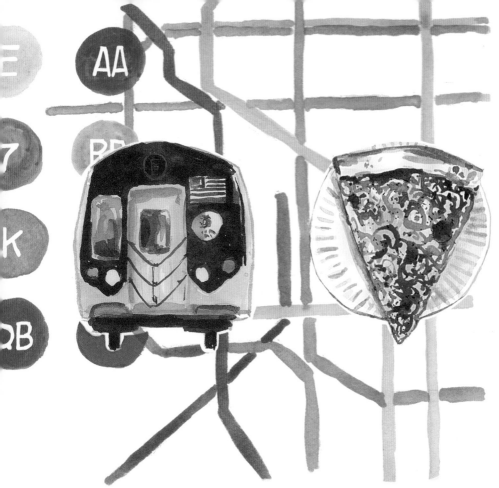

THE PIZZA PRINCIPLE

A mostly accurate "economic law" proposed by native New Yorker Eric M. Bram noted in 1980 that from the early 1960s "the price of a slice of pizza has matched, with uncanny precision, the cost of a New York subway ride." In 2014, a comprehensive analysis of subway fares and pizza slices performed by Columbia University statistics professor Jared Lander found the trend to be alive and well.

JOE'S

GRIMALDI'S

ROBERTA'S

NEW YORK BY THE SLICE

PRINCE STREET

DI FARA

TONY'S

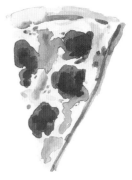

EMMY SQUARED

L'INDUSTRIE

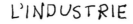

JULIANA'S

EMILY

ARCHIE'S

PATSY'S

BEST PIZZA

LUCALI'S

FORCELLA

PAULIE GEE'S

CROCODILE LOUNGE

free pizza with
every drink!

CALIFORNIA STYLE

Typically defined by combining New York- and Italian-style thin crust, with fresh, locally sourced toppings like fresh vegetables, fruits, and herbs.

ST. LOUIS STYLE

This style is marked by a thin crust made without yeast, and with pizzas cut into rectangles instead of wedges. In some cases, it's made with a soft, pasteurized processed cheese called **Provel**, which uses cheddar, Swiss, and provolone cheeses as flavorants. Not legally "cheese" under FDA guidelines.

IT'S almost CHEESE

CHICAGO STYLE

Invented in 1943 by Ric Riccardo, Ike Sewell, and chef Rudy Malnati at **Pizzeria Uno** in Chicago, this pizza is noted for its crust, which typically includes two signature ingredients: cornmeal and fat, usually butter or lard or both. Chicago style can be deep-dish, stuffed, pan, or even cracker thin "tavern style."

DETROIT STYLE

Invented in the 1940s by Gus Guerra of **Buddy's Rondezvous**, and originally made in heavy, square blue-steel pans, this pizza is rectangular and thick like a Sicilian pizza, but the cheese—Brick cheese, a high-fat aged cheese from Wisconsin—is piled very high up the sides of the pan to get the edges toasted and charred.

OLD FORGE PIZZA

Baked in rectangular metal trays, **Old Forge** pizza comes in two varieties: red or white. Red is made with tomato sauce and cheese; white is cheese only, double crust, with olive oil and rosemary sprinkled on top.

Welcome to
OLD FORGE, PA
PIZZA CAPITAL
of the **WORLD**

NEW HAVEN STYLE

Yale mascot
"Handsome Dan"

Originating at the Frank Pepe Pizzeria Napoletana, the "white clam pie" is made with crust, olive oil, oregano, grated Pecorino Romano cheese, chopped garlic, and fresh littleneck clams.

FRENCH BREAD PIZZA

ITHACA, NY, 1960—Bob Petrillose, founder of **The Hot Truck** food truck serving Cornell University, combined pizza sauce, fresh cheese and toppings, and French bread to create the "Poor Man's Pizza," or "PMP"—the first french bread pizza, which would become standard fare at school cafeterias across America.

PMP OPEN

The PMP was the (alleged) inspiration for Stouffer's French Bread Pizzas.

PESTO

Originating in Genoa, Italy, **pesto alla genovese** traditionally consists of crushed garlic, pine nuts, coarse salt, basil leaves, and a grated hard cheese like parmesan.

· GENOA ·

"Pesto" is derived from the Italian **pestare**, to pound, to crush. The same Latin root gave rise to the English noun **pestle**.

FRIED PIZZA

In war-torn Naples, "Pizza Fritta" became a trend as the impoverished working class struggled to make ends meet. Few could afford wood-fired ovens, and it was difficult to acquire ingredients like tomatoes and mozzarella, so people used cheaper alternatives like ricotta and pork fat.

In the 1954 film "L'oro di Napoli," Sophia Loren plays an unfaithful pizza maker who claims her missing jade ring fell into a mixture of fried pizza. "Pizza Fritta" lives on in the many "friggitorie" (fried food shops) of Naples.

PROVOL
POMODOR
2.00

THE THREE OFFICIAL VARIANTS

The **Associazione Verace Pizza Napoletana** recognizes three types of genuine Neapolitan pizzas: pizza Margherita, made with tomato, sliced mozzarella, basil, and extra-virgin olive oil; pizza Margherita extra, made with tomato, mozzarella from Campania in fillets, basil, and extra-virgin olive oil; and pizza marinara, made with tomato, garlic, oregano, and extra-virgin olive oil. The pizza napoletana is a Traditional Speciality Guaranteed (TSG) product in Europe.

pizza marinara

pizza margherita

pizza margherita extra

53

ROMAN STYLES

pizzetta

"Pizza al taglio"
(Pizza by the cut)
is cut with scissors
to the customer's
desired size.

pizza con funghi

pizza margherita alla pala

SICILIAN PIZZA

With its roots in **pizza in teglia**—a pan pizza popular in Puglia and southern Italy—the Sicilian American version is a fluffy, rectangular pan pizza similar to focaccia. Ideally, it's made in an iron or steel pan with generous amounts of olive oil.

Sicilian American
Joe DiMaggio

PIZZA BIANCA

The less-is-more pizza. Olive oil. Salt. Simple.
Can be pillowy soft, or **scrocchiarella** (crunchy).
Ubiquitous in Rome, it's popular at places like
Panificio Filli Passi and Forno Campo de' Fiori.

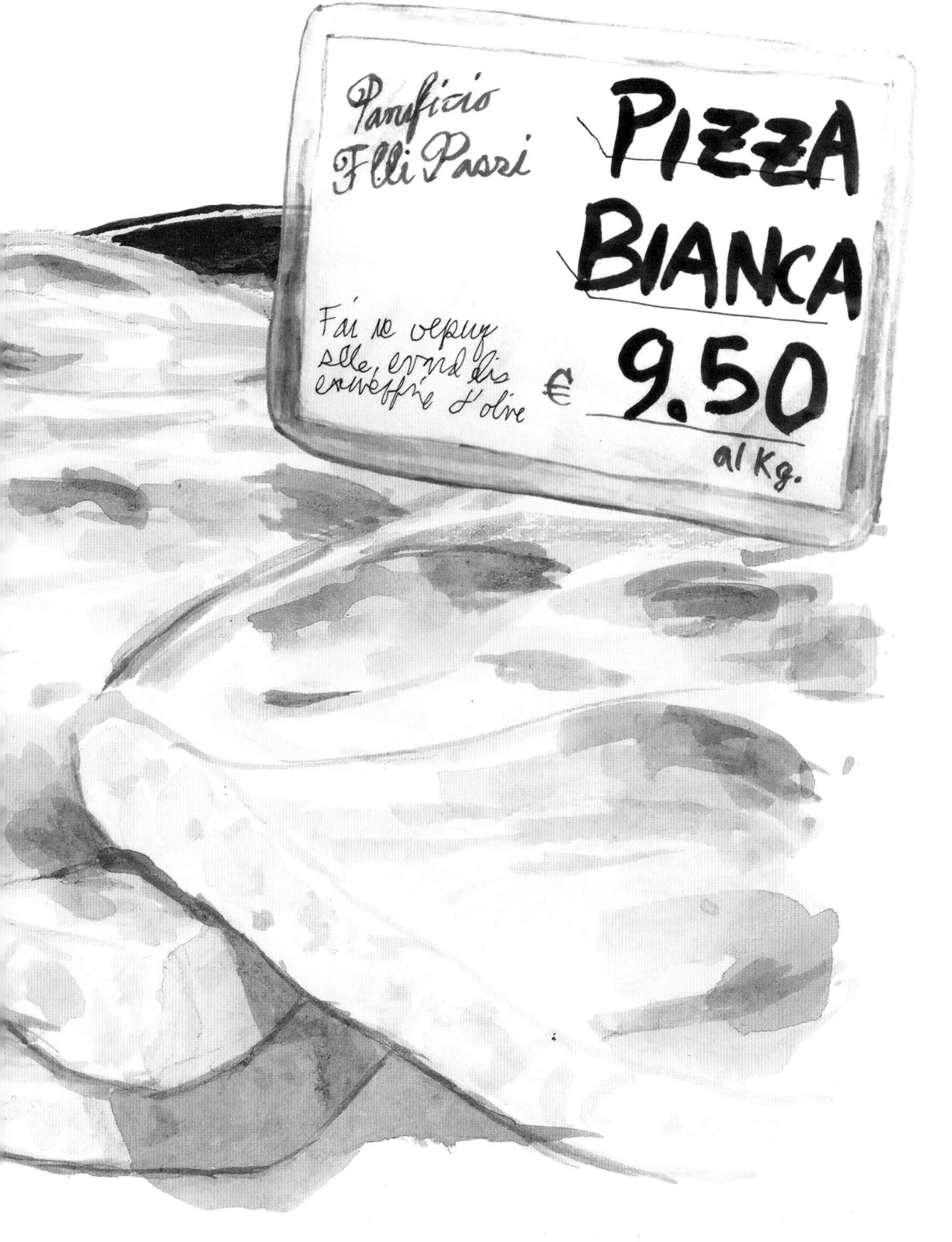
Panificio
F.lli Passi
PIZZA
BIANCA
€ 9.50
al Kg.

TRAPIZZINO

POLPETTA
AL SUGO

An invention of Roman restaurateur Stefano Callegari in 2008, the trapizzino reimagines the classic pizza slice as a thick, triangular **pizza bianca** sliced open and filled with a variety of ingredients. The name derives from a play on words, combining **tramezzino** (a triangular sandwich served in cafes in Italy) and **pizza**.

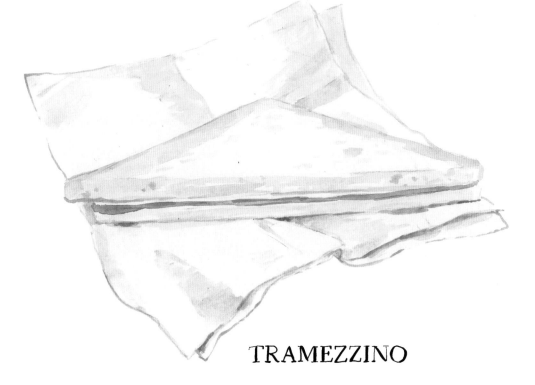

TRAMEZZINO

THINGS THAT

Stromboli

Calzone

AREN'T PIZZA

Bruschetta & Crostini

Meatball sandwich

For better or for worse, **pizza** vending machines are popping up in colleges, hospitals, and malls around the world.

Salt Lake City, Utah

Chatswood, NSW, Australia

Xavier University, Cincinnati, Ohio

Cologne, Germany

BAGEL BITES

"Pizza in the morning,
Pizza in the evenin',
Pizza at suppertime!
When pizza's on a bagel,
You can eat pizza anytime!"

— 1990s TV commercial jingle

67

ANATOMY

The components of pizza, from the tools that make it to the seasonings that complete it.

TOOLS of the TRADE

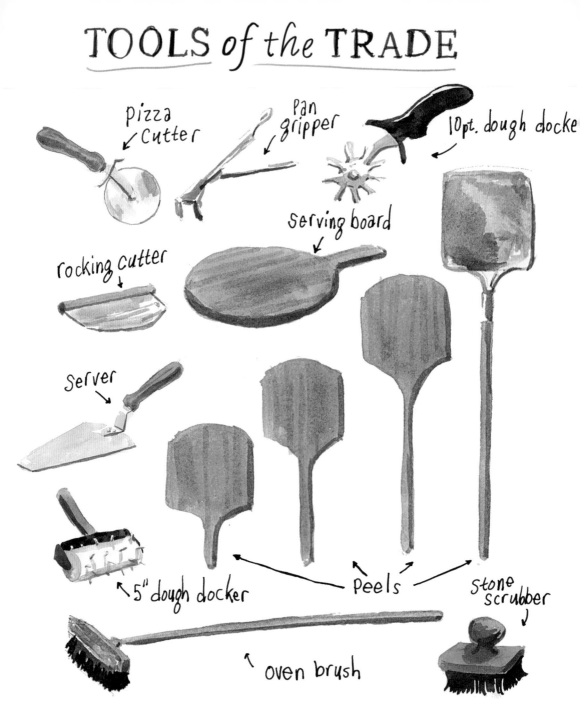

Pizza Cutter

Pan gripper

10pt. dough docker

serving board

rocking cutter

Server

5" dough docker

Peels

stone scrubber

oven brush

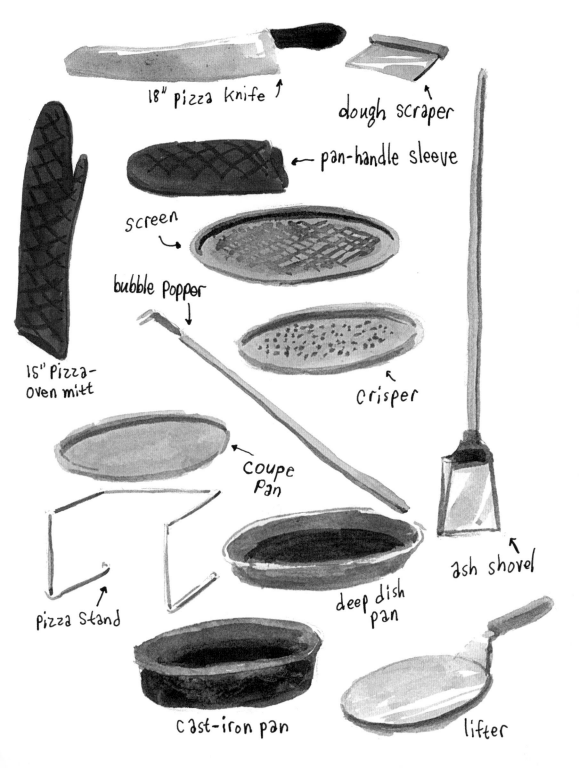

18" pizza knife

dough scraper

pan-handle sleeve

screen

bubble popper

crisper

15" pizza-oven mitt

coupe pan

ash shovel

pizza stand

deep dish pan

cast-iron pan

lifter

FLOUR

ALL-PURPOSE FLOUR

Good for most pizza recipes, but the dough may tear more easily. Suitable for Sicilian and deep-dish crusts and will also do well with thin-crust pizza styles.

BREAD FLOUR

Easy to find, affordable, and adds some crispness to thin-crust and New York-style pizzas—making the crust crispy on the outside and chewy and textured inside.

"00" FLOUR

For Neapolitan-style pizza, which is thin in the middle and puffs up around the rim. This fine grind, along with a 12.5% gluten content, gives the dough the right elasticity.

READY, SET, Dough!

salt

olive oil

water

active dry yeast

flour

baking soda

73

NEAPOLITAN-STYLE CRUST

Characterized by a thin layer of crispness to the crust, followed by an interior that is moist, poofy, and cloud-like. It can appear leopard-spotted, with many small dark spots surrounded by paler dough. True Neapolitan pies are not stiff—you can't pick them up as a slice. A fork and knife are perfectly acceptable.

poofy goodness!

NEW YORK-STYLE CRUST

New York-style is an offshoot of Neapolitan-style, designed to be cooked in slightly cooler-burning coal-fired/gas-fired ovens. It's stretched out slightly thicker than a Neapolitan base, though on the scale of pizzas, it's still considered "thin crust."

SICILIAN-STYLE CRUST

A variation of New York-style, it's baked in a tray loaded with olive oil. As it bakes, the bottom of the pie essentially fries, coming out ultra-crisp, maintaining a puffy interior.

DOUGH THROW

Throwing dough is the best way to stretch it without the damage of pushing it with your fingers. Tossing pizza dough in the air also helps ensure the correct amount of moisture, as the airflow over the dough's surface dries it out just enough to make it less sticky and easier to handle.

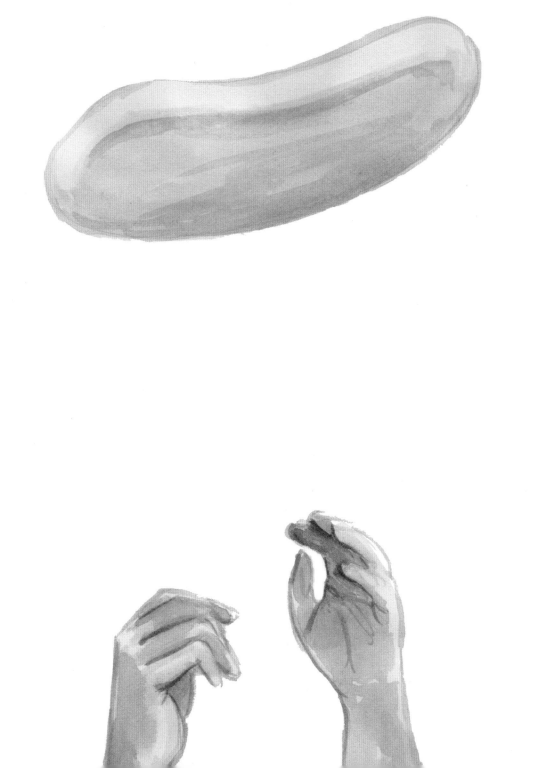

PIZZA CHEESE

Mozzarella
Globally, the most popular
pizza cheese

Provolone
Second most popular,
often mixed with mozzarella

Parmesan
Finely grated topping,
doesn't melt well

The most popular cheeses used
for pizza are mozzarella, provolone,
cheddar, and parmesan; Emmental,
Pecorino, and ricotta are often used
as toppings; and processed pizza
cheeses manufactured specifically
for pizza are used often in mass-
production environments.

Pecorino
Hard, salty, made
from sheep's milk

Ricotta
Added as a topping

Cheddar
Mixed with mozzarella
to prevent blistering
of pizza cheese

Emmental
Added as a topping

Provel
Processed cheese, used
in St. Louis-style pizza

BUFFALO MOZZARELLA

The term "mozzarella" derives from the procedure called mozzare, which means "cutting by hand," separating from the curd, and serving in individual pieces.

PASTA FILATA (spun paste)

The curd is mixed and kneaded until the required soft, elastic, stringy texture is obtained. The mass of curd is divided often by pulling out a thick strand and then chopping and shaping it into individual cheeses.

?

TOMATO SAUCE

Typical Neapolitan pizza sauce is made with San Marzano tomatoes, an Italian heirloom variety of plum tomatoes first grown in volcanic soils near Mount Vesuvius. Their thicker juice, meaty interior, and lower acidity makes them ideal for creating an uncooked sauce.

TOPPINGS

mushrooms

pepperoni

potatoes

sausage

There's no shortage of choices
when it comes to personalizing
a pizza. Options range from
the beloved pepperoni to the
downright polarizing pineapple.

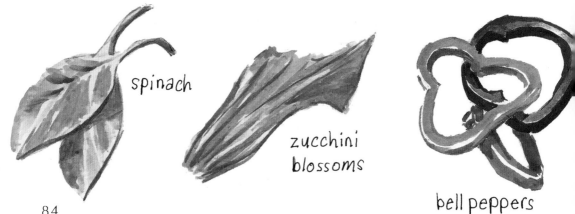

spinach

zucchini
blossoms

bell peppers

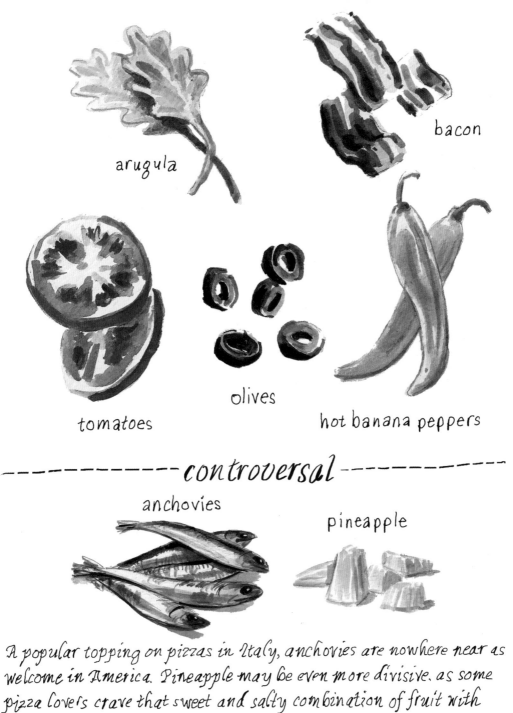

arugula

bacon

tomatoes

olives

hot banana peppers

-------------------- controversal --------------------

anchovies

pineapple

A popular topping on pizzas in Italy, anchovies are nowhere near as welcome in America. Pineapple may be even more divisive, as some pizza lovers crave that sweet and salty combination of fruit with melted cheese, while others find the pairing objectionable.

PEPPERONI

America's favorite topping, it's estimated that 36% of pizza sold in the U.S. is topped with pepperoni.

This topping is **not** actually Italian. The word "pepperoni" is a borrowing from **peperoni**, the plural of **peperone**, Italian for **bell pepper**. The sausage we know as pepperoni is an Italo-American invention dating back to the 1930s.

Inspired by spicy Italian sausage, the Americanized version uses **beef**, an ingredient not often found in sausage in Italy, but common in America. It's the beef fat that helps the pepperoni withstand the high heat of a pizza oven.

SEASONINGS

pepper

garlic powder (not salt)

red pepper flakes

oregano

grated parmesan

The customization of a pizza concludes with the addition of seasonings, which can nudge the overall taste toward the spicy and hot (red pepper flakes) or toward the sweet and herbal (fresh basil).

fresh basil

thyme

paprika

fennel
seeds

LEFTOVERS

Remnant anecdotes, innovations, and
observations—from the inherent truth
about all pizzas to the ovens and pizzerias
that make them.

"Every pizza is a personal pizza if you try hard enough and believe in yourself."

～ Bill Murray

WORLD'S LARGEST PIZZA

Made in Rome in December 2012, it was named "Ottavia" in honor of the first Roman emperor, Octavian Augustus. The pizza measured 131 feet in diameter and weighed in at 25.6 tons.

INGREDIENTS:
19,800 lbs of flour • 10,000 lbs of tomato sauce
8,800 lbs of mozzarella cheese
1,488 lbs of margarine
551 lbs of rock salt

PIZZA PRANK

AMHERST, MA — Shortly after a Bob Dylan concert at the University of Massachusets in 2010, a man wearing a Dylan backstage pass around his neck ordered $3,900 worth of pizzas from Antonio's Pizza, promising to deliver them to Dylan's crew and a big tip upon his return. He never came back. The prankster eventually fessed up to the expensive caper, and agreed to pay for the 178 pizzas. Dylan was cleared of all charges.

SPECIAL DELIVERY

Domino's employees may have saved a man's life. When workers didn't hear from one of their regular customers for several days, they sent one of their drivers, Tracey Hamblen, to check on him. The man didn't answer the door but the lights and TV were on, so Hamblen called 911. When deputies responded to the man's home, they heard someone calling for help. They found the man on the ground and in need of medical attention. The customer had been ordering a pizza almost every day for more than 10 years.

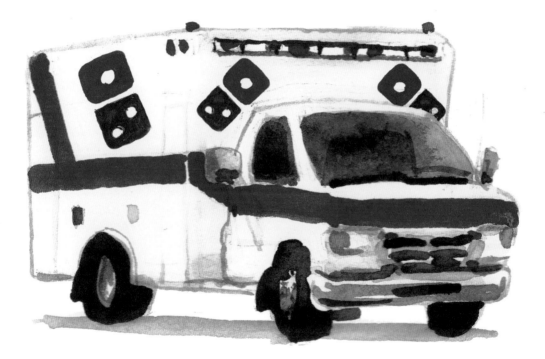

3-D PRINTED PIZZA

In 2013, an Austin, Texas, start-up, BeeHex, was commissioned by NASA to develop a device to make pizza—as opposed to normal unappetizing space food—for future Mars missions. Pizza is a strong candidate for 3-D printing because all of its components can be printed individually, layer by layer. Even though the printer was successful, budget cuts would force NASA to shelve the project.

DRONE DELIVERY

WHANGAPARAOA, N.Z., 2016 – Domino's Pizza delivers
the world's first-ever pizza-by-drone. The **Peri-Peri Chicken**
and **Chicken and Cranberry** pizzas touched down in the
backyard of Emma and Johnny Norman after a flight of
less than five minutes. The hope, according to Domino's
GM of New Zealand Scott Bush, is for all of the company's
deliveries there to be done by drones within the next few **years.**

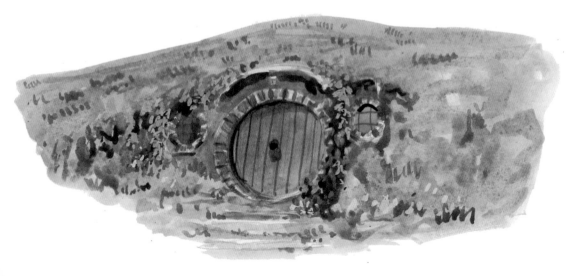

$\sqrt{PIZZA}$ MATH

SOLVING for VOLUME

radius: z

thickness: a

$$V = \pi z^2 a$$

$$V = Pi(z*z)a$$

HOW MANY PIZZAS TO ORDER?

This equation assumes that a typical pizza is cut into eight slices, and that a hungry person would eat three slices.

$$X * \,^3/_8 = P$$

$X =$ 👥 (# of guests)

$P =$ 🍕 (# of pizzas)

Eugenia Cheng, a mathematician with the University of Sheffield, figured out a formula for creating the perfect pizza:

$$\frac{t}{d} \cdot \frac{r^6}{(r^3 - 15)^2}$$

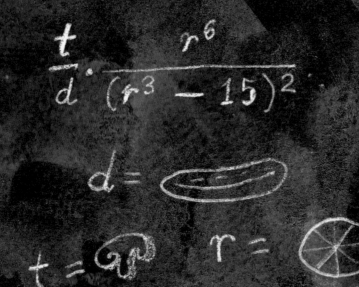

$$d = $$

$$t = \qquad r = $$

Her formula uses "t" to designate the constant volume of toppings, "d" to designate the constant volume of dough, and "r" for radius. The formula allows for a comparison of the amount of toppings in an average bite across different sizes of pizza.

• MONOHEDRAL DISC TILING •

Mathematicians from the University of Liverpool have developed new geometric designs that can be used to cut a pizza into equally sized slices.

Joel Haddley and Stephen Worsley expanded on a previous design that shows it is possible to cut a pizza into twelve identical pieces by first cutting six curved pieces, and then slicing those in half. In mathematics, this process is known as monohedral disc tiling.

By changing the original curved slices into shapes with an odd number of straight sides, one can make more complex patterns with equally sized pieces. The shapes of the slices are referred to by the number of straight sides they have, "5-gons," "7-gons," "9-gons," etc. A circle can be infinitely divided up this way into smaller and smaller segments.

·INVENTIONS·

ROTARY KNIFE

No. 630,094.

W. L. NOBLE.
ROTARY KNIFE.
(Application filed July 31, 1897)

Patented Aug. 1, 1899

(No Model)

Fig. 1

4,441,626

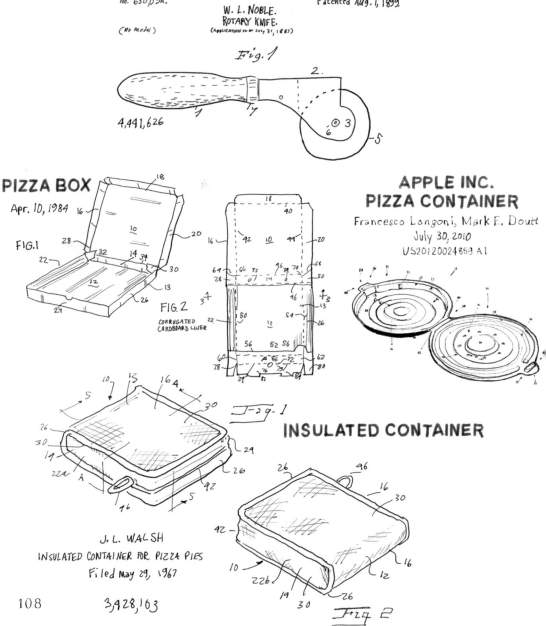

PIZZA BOX

Apr. 10, 1984

FIG.1

FIG.2

CORRUGATED
CARDBOARD LINER

APPLE INC.
PIZZA CONTAINER

Francesco Longoni, Mark E. Doutt
July 30, 2010
US20120024859 A1

INSULATED CONTAINER

J. L. WALSH

INSULATED CONTAINER FOR PIZZA PIES

Filed May 29, 1967

108   3,428,163

THE PLASTIC THINGY

Carmela Vitale from Dix Hills, New York, filed her patent (#4,498,586) for "The Pizza Saver" on February 10, 1983, and got it issued on February 12, 1985. The tiny tripod provides support to a potential sagging pizza-box lid. It is placed in the middle of the pie to maintain the structural integrity of the box.

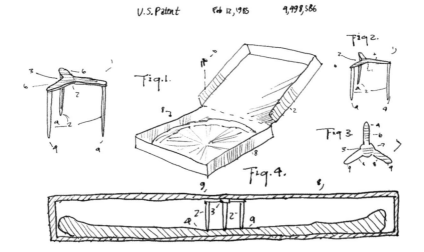

U.S. Patent   Feb 12, 1985   4,498,586

Fig.1.

Fig 2.

Fig 3.

Fig.4.

OTHER PIZZA SAVERS

EAMES EIFFEL TABLE

ROBOTIC PIZZA

MOUNTAIN VIEW, CA—Inside the pizza chain **Zume Pizza**, pizza dough travels down a conveyor belt where machines add and spread the sauce and later carefully slide the uncooked pies into an 800-degree oven.

Isaac Asimov's
THREE LAWS
of PIZZA ROBOTICS

FIRST LAW

A pizza robot may not burn a pizza or, through inaction, allow a pizza to come to harm.

SECOND LAW

A pizza robot must accept orders for pizzas except where such orders would conflict with the First Law.

THIRD LAW

A pizza robot must protect its own recipes as long as such protection does not conflict with the First or Second Laws.

Naples

Rome

The neighborhood pizzeria comes in all shapes and sizes, with no shortage of inventive offerings, from **pizza fritta** to **pizza pot pie**.

Philadelphia

San Francisco

Chicago

New York

PIZZA
POT
PIE

The widespread use, all over the world, of vehicles to serve pizza to people attests to the fact that pizza is both mobile and global.

Wrocław, Poland

London, England

Fujisawa, Kanagawa, Japan

San Francisco, California

Cusco, Peru

Portland, Oregon

Newcastle Upon Tyne, England

Vancouver, BC, Canada

Dallas, Texas

Pizza ovens are every bit as personalized as the pizzas they make. Whether it's a backyard wood-fired oven or a counter-top electric model, there's an oven for any situation.

117

PIZZA HUT
ELECTRIC
BAKING OVEN
(1975–1976)

pizza oven and fixin's   **10.99**

Mama mia! Even youngsters can make real pizza! Famous Pizza Hut® mini oven cooks with heat from one 60W bulb (not incl.) Comes with dough and sauce mix for 6 pizzas, 2 baking pans, and serving paddle like a real pizzeria. Put up the "official" sign and you're in business! Plastic; 12x7½ x16½ in. hi. Ages 8, up.

N57 J 6377—UL listed; 110-120V, AC. Mailable. (5 lbs.) . . . . .Set 10.99

N57 J 6021—REFILL—Paddle plus 2 pans, mixes for 24 pizzas. (13 oz.). 4.99

ACKNOWLEDGMENTS

MOM DAD
JERRY SARAH MARY
TOMMY JOHNNY
COLLEEN MAUREEN

JENNY WAPNER
KATE WOODROW
ANGELINA CHENEY
LISA FERKEL
BETSY STROMBERG
ALICE CHAU

REFERENCES

THE PIZZA BIBLE

DELIZIA! THE EPIC HISTORY
OF THE ITALIANS AND THEIR FOOD

SMITHSONIAN MAGAZINE

THE WASHINGTON POST

BUSINESS INSIDER

THE HOME PIZZERIA

THE HISTORY CHANNEL

EATER

SERIOUS EATS

HOWSTUFFWORKS

NEWSCIENTIST

ASSOUPASPOSSIBLE

GUINNESSWORLDRECORDS

PUBLISHED IN THE UNITED STATES BY TEN SPEED PRESS, AN IMPRINT OF THE CROWN PUBLISHING GROUP, A DIVISION OF PENGUIN RANDOM HOUSE LLC, NEW YORK.
WWW.CROWNPUBLISHING.COM
WWW.TENSPEED.COM

TEN SPEED PRESS AND THE TEN SPEED PRESS COLOPHON ARE REGISTERED TRADEMARKS OF PENGUIN RANDOM HOUSE LLC.

LIBRARY OF CONGRESS CATALOGING-IN-PUBLICATION DATA IS ON FILE WITH THE PUBLISHER.

HARDCOVER ISBN: 978-0-399-57997-4
EBOOK ISBN: 978-0-399-57998-1

PRINTED IN CHINA

DESIGN BY ANGELINA CHENEY AND LISA FERKEL

10 9 8 7 6 5 4 3 2 1

FIRST EDITION

MADE IN SAN FRANCISCO • CHICAGO • NEW YORK • NAPLES • ROME

"Not everyone's going to like me. I'm not pizza."
— *Anonymous*